Killer Bunnies

Killer Bunnies

by Charles Bordin

St. Martin's Press, New York

Library of Congress Cataloguing in Publication Data
Bordin, Charles.
  Killer bunnies.

    1. American wit and humor, Pictorial.
I. Title.
NC1429.B668A4   1982   741.5'973   81-14
ISBN 0-312-45341-8   AACR2

have you seen your bunny
standing in the shadows?

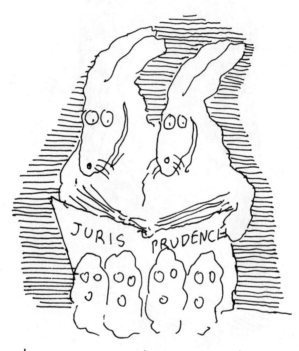

bunnies laugh at the law

a broccoli grows in brooklyn

fox holding up dry cleaner
while rabbit cuts the wires

what the rabbit bit

bunnies selling bennies

rabbit waiting for the
statute of limitations to
run out.

Bunnies are well adapted by nature
to the profession of safecracker

nobody knows the bunnies I
have seen.

bent bunnies

NO BUNNY HOME.

bird envying a mammal

rabbit plotting escape by
whittling gun out of wood

rabbit violating postal regulations

bunny pretending to be
docile. (motive: lettuce)

woman throwing over her career
for her bunny

cote d'rabbit
(where to go after a successful
embezzlement.)

rabbits who have kept their
hutch insurance premiums paid up.

rabbit fighting extradition

outlaw bunny wondering which
law to break next

rabbit signing pledge of vegetarianism
in front of committee of chickens

rabbit filing for bankruptcy

bunny crouching low and keeping ears
down so as to get a free bus ride

bunny feeding a slug to a
vending machine

vegetables fleeing the approach
of a horde of bunnies

rabbit thinking up a flowery
speech full of excuses

bunny hiding from bloodhounds
after escape from chain gang.

This rabbit is a picket fence

Guilty rabbit pleading Not Guilty

rabbit redeemed

Bunny learning how to be a hop-scotch hustler

rabbit denying parole to a hamster

rabbit slipping cat a fin to
keep quiet.

rabbit goosing a sunflower

bunnies facing reality

Bunny slippers sliding past
cop.

The Broccoli Cover-up.

broccoli escaping detection by disguising itself as a christmas tree.

Rabbit who is dissatisfied with his lot.

Rabbits opening their checks
from the League for Animal Welfare

bunnies deploring the recent
decline in spiritual values

rabbits are only after one thing

Raccoon robbing Peter to pay a rabbit

rabbit and henchrabbit

rabbit being turned away from
home for wanting to marry a
turnip.

rabbit getting some juice, on the pad

rabbit selling prints

rabbit being bothered
by scruples.

pampered greenhouse plants watching
horror film

rabbit luring a wild broccoli
with a handful of plant food

Bunny who is a shrewd marble trader

Seed pods rehearsing scene
from "Invasion of the Bunny Snatchers."

Nice bunnies don't
look down on people

A Bunny With Ideas

Broccoli giving themselves
up for Lent.

Waiter, there's a bunny in
my soup

Bunny telling broccoli to
be philosophical

Selfish rabbit refusing to
share with rabid shellfish

dirty old bunny broadcasting propaganda
near school.

rabbit trying to hustle a
cat for affection

rabbit collared with collard

a rabbit on alice lands

Broccoli and grouse writing to
the New York Times to complain
about bunnies.

Vicious animal being
tamed by the power of
affection

Bunny giving short weight
to a nitrates buyer

A rather tolerant rabbit

bunny with lynx to the
intelligence community

rowf

rabbit grousing at a carp

Bunnies reading grouse's diary
during the mating season

nasty rabbit in a cute pose

Bunnies toasting bagels

Bunny cast in a negative light

this rabbit didn't see
nothin' and don't know
nothin'

well, so much for rabbits